BEDTIME PARABLES

VOLUME 1

Bill Dodds

Our Sunday Visitor Publishing Division
Our Sunday Visitor, Inc.
Huntington, Indiana 46750

ISBN: 0-87973-570-8 (hardcover)
ISBN: 0-87973-569-4 (softcover)
LCCCN: 92-61549

PRINTED IN THE UNITED STATES OF AMERICA

Cover and text illustrations by James E. McIlrath

TO WILL JOHNSON AND SARAH PETRICH,
WITH LOVE FROM YOUR GODFATHER

Sammy the Samaritan Makes a New Friend

Bop!

"Ouch!" cried Wally Walker as a rock the size of an egg bounced off his head and landed near his feet.

Wally had been on his way from the big city of Jerusalem to the not-so-big city of Jericho fifteen miles away when a stone came sailing out of the clear blue sky and beaned him.

He looked up the road.

And he looked down the road.

But he couldn't see anyone.

"Now, where do you suppose. . . ?" he started to ask.

Bop!

"Ouch!"

Another one.

"Hey, cut that out!" he yelled.

Bop!

"Ouch! Hey. . ."

Bop! Bop! Bop!

"Ouch! Ouch! Ouch!"

Now poor Wally had six lumps and was starting to feel very, very dizzy. "I think I better sit down," he said to himself, "before I fall down."

Plop! He sat down, right in the middle of the dirt road.

Bop! A seventh rock hit him.

"Oooh!" he kind of groaned and sort of moaned and fell back in the dirt.

Wally closed his eyes and lay still and then he heard three men's voices.

"He's out," said the first one.

"Sure is," the second agreed.

"I get his cloak," the third one shouted, meaning the cape Wally was wearing for a coat.

"My cloak?" Wally thought. "These three men are . . . ROBBERS!"

He opened his eyes a teeny-tiny bit and watched as two huge men and one little fellow came around from behind a giant boulder next to the road. Then he quickly shut his eyes as the men crept closer.

"I get his money," the first man said, reaching down and pulling a small

5

pouch from Wally's belt. "Let's see what we have here. Oh-ho! Pieces of silver. One, two, three. All for me."

"I get his robe and his sandals," the second one said, pulling off Wally's shoes and the robe he was wearing.

"I get his cloak!" the third one, the small man, reminded the other two. "Look!" he cried, trying it on. "A perfect fit!"

Wally opened his eyes again. One robber was counting silver coins. One was looking at Wally's sandals. And one was trying on his cloak. "A perfect fit," the little fellow said again, although he was so short the cloak dragged in the dust behind him.

Wally couldn't help laughing a little laugh because the third robber looked so silly.

"He's awake!" the little man told the others.

"Can't have that," the first one said.

Smack!

Whack!

Crack!

Each robber hit poor Wally and then they went on their way.

A little bit later, a local leader came down the road. He was dressed in fine, fine clothes and riding a fat gray donkey. "Thank you, thank you, I thank you," the leader was saying out loud to himself. People were always telling the leader how wonderful he was and he needed to be ready to answer.

"Thank you, thank you, I thank. . ." He pulled the reins and stopped his donkey. There, in the middle of the road, was a man without a robe or sandals or cloak and he had bumps all over his head.

"Help me. . ." Wally Walker said weakly.

"Thank you, thank you, I thank you. Thank you, thank you, I thank you," the leader said quickly, tapping his heels into the sides of the chubby animal. He lowered his head, pretending not to see Wally, and rode by as fast as he could. "Thank you, thank you, I. . ." his voice trailed off.

And very soon he was gone.

A little later Wally spotted someone from his own part of town walking toward him. The man was singing:

"It's a beautiful day,
and I'm here to say,
it's all because
God made it this way!"

"Hey," Wally called out, but it was barely above a whisper. The man stopped and looked down. A lump in the middle of the road was talking to him! "Please, help me," Wally said.

The man's eyes grew big and his mouth fell open. Then he blinked twice, snapped his mouth shut, and scurried around poor Wally Walker.

Later still — a lot later, not a little later —   Wally saw another person coming down the road. He was riding a very small donkey. So small that the man's feet almost touched the ground. "Whoa!" the man said to his animal when he saw Wally. "Uh-oh."

The man slid off his donkey and grabbed a canteen of water. "Here," he said kneeling next to Wally. He lifted Wally's head a bit and let him take a long, cool drink.

The water tasted *so* good!

"You're a . . . Samaritan!" Wally said. He was very surprised. "You're not from around here. You're from Samaria. My people and your people don't like each other. Why would you. . . ?"

"Sammy the Samaritan, at your service," the man said. "You look like you could use some help."

Wally nodded. "Ouch," he said again because nodding made his head hurt more. "Robbers did this."

Then Sammy gently dabbed at Wally's bumps with a damp cloth and got some bandages to cover them. He helped Wally get up on the little donkey and walked beside him until they reached an inn.

Sammy rented a room for the night and took care of Wally. The next day he told the innkeeper, "I have to leave now, but here is some money for the room and for food and for you to take very good care of my new friend Wally until he feels better. I'll stop by later and, if this isn't enough money, I'll give you more then."

Then Sammy went outside and climbed on his donkey. He looked back at the inn and there, in the window, was Wally. Wally smiled and waved and then Sammy smiled and waved, too, and headed down the road again.

A Little Bedtime Prayer

Jesus, thank you for people I know who are like Sammy the Samaritan. People who help me when I'm hurt or when I feel sad or mad or scared. Help me be like Sammy because he was like you. And someday, Jesus, I would like to ride a little donkey. Amen.

Grown-up Stuff

The parable of the good Samaritan can be found in Luke's gospel, chapter 10, verses 29-37. Jesus told this story after a scholar asked him what a person needed to do to gain eternal life. Christ answered, "What does the law say?" and the man replied, "Love God and love your neighbor."

"That's right," Jesus said and then the scholar asked, "But who is my neighbor?" There has to be a loophole here somewhere!

Then Jesus told this parable. It wasn't a priest or a Levite — leaders in the local community — who stopped to help but a Samaritan. Samaria was the land between Judea (in the south) and Galilee (in the north) that was west of the Jordan River. The Jews and Samaritans were ethnic and religious foes.

After Jesus finished his story, he asked the scholar, "Which of these three was neighbor to the man who was robbed?" The scholar answered, "The one who was kind," and Jesus told him, "Go and do likewise."

The Shepherd With One Hundred Sheep

"Good morning, sheep," said the shepherd as the sun peeked out from behind a hill and he pulled his cloak a little tighter around himself. "You're very lucky animals. It's cold this morning, but you always have your warm wool sweaters."

"Baa," answered a few of the one hundred sheep milling about in the pen beside the barn where they slept each night.

" 'Bah'? " the shepherd replied. "What do you mean 'bah'? It's the truth!"

Now the shepherd knew sheep can't *really* talk. He just liked to pretend. The truth was he loved his sheep and his sheep seemed to love him, too.

"How did you sleep last night?" the shepherd asked them.

"Baa," the fluffy animals complained.

"Bad? You slept bad?" the shepherd said. "I'm so sorry to hear that. I slept very well. I am ready for a long, full day of shepherding."

"Baa-baa."

"Of course we'll take the babies with us. Don't we always take the lambs? We'll take *all* the sheep. The old ones, like Bubba, here." He pointed at a tired, old ram — a boy sheep — with curly horns. "The middle-aged ones, like the twins, Babs and Beth. The teenagers, like . . . like . . . Now what are their names again?"

"Baa," the sheep said.

"What? Oh, you're giving me a hint, are you?"

"Baa."

"B? Their names start with a B? Hmmm . . . Well, anyway, the teens and the babies, too."

"Baa-baa."

"Did I just say the babies, too? Come on, now." He opened the pen's gate just a bit and started to count as the sheep slipped through.

"One, two, three, four," he counted. "Five, six, seven, eight."

He stopped. Babs and Beth were trying to push through the small opening at the same time, but they couldn't both fit.

"Ladies, ladies, ladies," the shepherd said. "Don't I always tell you 'one at a time'? Now whose turn is it to go first?"

" 'Babs,' " Babs seemed to say.

" 'Beth!' " the shepherd was sure Beth had shouted.

"Oh, all right. Let's see. Where was I? One, two, three . . . Uh. One, two, three . . . four! Okay. Five, six, seven . . . Five, six, seven . . . Five, six, seven, *eight!*" He opened the gate just a little bit wider so both sheep could fit through at the same time. "Nine-ten!" he said quickly and closed the gate back up a bit again.

"One, two, three, *four!* Five, six, seven, *eight!* Nine-ten," the shepherd repeated and yawned a great yawn and then shook his head very fast. "I don't know why this always makes me so *sleepy!*"

Then he laughed as if that had to be the funniest joke in the world. He knew that some people say that when they can't fall asleep, they pretend to count sheep and that makes them very, very sleepy. So every morning he counted to ten ("One, two, three, four. Five, six, seven, eight. Nine-ten!"). And every morning he yawned a great yawn and shook his head very fast and said, "I don't know why this always makes me so *sleepy!*" And then he finished counting his sheep. Which is exactly what he did on this fine, cool morning.

"Eleven, twelve, thirteen. . ."

"Thirty-one, thirty-two, thirty-three. . ."

"Sixty-six, sixty-seven, sixty-eight. . ."

All the way up to "Ninety-eight, ninety-nine, one hundred!" And off he went. Walking ahead as his one hundred sheep followed.

The shepherd and his sheep spent the day — as they spent all their days — on some lovely green hills. The sheep wandered about and ate grass. The older ones napped and the younger ones chased each other and went exploring. The shepherd listened to birds and watched rabbits and squirrels and made sure no wolf crept in to harm his sheep.

Then, toward the end of the afternoon, he announced, "It's time to sing! What shall we sing?"

"Baa-baa," said the sheep.

"A baby song? All right. Let's sing 'Rock-a-bye, Baby.' Remember, I need your help now. Ready? I'll begin." He cleared his throat — "Hmmff, hmmff" — and he sang:

"Rock-a-bye. . ."

"Baa-baa," the sheep said.

". . .on the treetop. When the wind. . ."

"Baa."

". . .the cradle will rock. When the. . ."

"Baa."

". . .breaks, the cradle will fall, and down will come. . ."

"Baa-baa."

". . .cradle and all."

Then the shepherd clapped his hands and said, "Very good!" and the sheep ate a little more grass. By now the sun was setting and dark fat clouds — that looked a great deal like stout black sheep — were rolling in, and so the shepherd said, "It's time to head for home."

The sun was almost gone by the time they reached the sheep pen and barn and it had started to rain. Giant drops that went *Plop!* on the shepherd's head and the sheep's noses.

The shepherd opened the pen's gate a tiny bit and counted as the sheep quickly entered one at a time. (Except for Babs and Beth.) "Ninety-seven, ninety-eight, ninety-nine. Uh-oh."

He let them back out. "Ninety-seven, ninety-eight, ninety-nine." And he let them back in. "Ninety-seven, ninety-eight, ninety-nine."

One of his sheep was missing! One of his sheep was lost!

It was raining hard now and it was very dark except when the lightning cracked — *Crackle, crackle, crackle!* And then the thunder rolled — *Boom, boom, boom!* But the shepherd ran back to the hill where he and his sheep had spent the day and he searched and he searched and he searched.

"Baa. . ."

Did he hear something? He stopped and listened.

Crackle, crackle, crackle! Boom, boom, boom!

"Baa. . ."

There it was! A baby boy sheep. It had wandered off a bit too far and its short fleece was caught in some thorny bramble bushes.

"Ah-ha!" said the shepherd as he scooped up the little sheep and cradled the very frightened and very wet animal in his arms. The shepherd slipped the lamb under his cloak and danced and sang all the way home. He set the lamb over the fence into the pen and watched as it scooted into the barn to be with the others.

By this time the storm was over and the shepherd called his neighbors together and said, "We're going to have a party! I lost my little lamb, but now

13

I've found him!" His neighbors and friends were as happy as he was and they danced and they sang all night long with him.

A Little Bedtime Prayer

Jesus, you're the Good Shepherd. Thank you for always watching over all your sheep, even little lambs like me. I think it would be fun to sing "Rock-a-bye, Baby" with a sheep. Amen.

Grown-up Stuff

Jesus told this parable (Luke 15:1-7) after some Pharisees and scribes had complained. (Pharisees and scribes were hotshots who were sticklers for enforcing the letter, but not necessarily the spirit, of the law.) They were commenting that Jesus "welcomes sinners and eats with them," and so he told them the story of the shepherd and the one hundred sheep. Then he said to them, "In the same way, there will be more joy in heaven over one sinner who repents than over ninety-nine righteous people who have no need for repentance."

In the same chapter, Luke follows up with the parable of the woman who lost a coin and the well-known story of the prodigal son. All three parables show Christ's concern for those who are lost and the special love God has for sinners who come back to him.

The parable of the one hundred sheep can also be found in Matthew (18:12-14). Here there is an emphasis on the importance of not leading "little ones" astray and the duty of helping those who are lost find their way back "into the fold."

The Ten Young Women With the Little Lamps

"Just look at the size of that house!" said Anna as she tilted her head back and stared at the huge building. Anna's nine friends looked up, too.

They looked up and up.

And up and up and up.

And up and up and up and up, until one woman named Betty leaned back so far she fell right over.

Whump!

"That," said Betty as she sat on the ground and pointed toward the roof, "is a big house."

And all the women laughed.

"Did you break your lamp?" Anna asked Betty.

Did she break her lamp? What a silly question. When someone falls down and goes *whump!*, a friend usually says, "Are you all right?" or "Did you hurt yourself?" Not "Did you break your lamp?"

But Betty and Anna and the other young women didn't think this was a silly question. These ten women were dressed in their finest clothes and each was carrying a little clay lamp that didn't use electricity or batteries or kerosene. These lamps used oil.

Anna and Betty and the others had been chosen to wait outside this big beautiful house for a bridegroom who was coming that night. This was his house and they would be outside by the front door to say, "Welcome, welcome, welcome!"

The women knew they had a very important job. They knew that when a bridegroom is coming to his big beautiful house, you can't just leave the front porch light on.

"Did you break your lamp?" Anna asked again.

"No," said Betty, as two friends helped her up. "My lamp is fine." She held up the tiny clay pot. "But my seat is a little sore." And all the ladies laughed again.

Then, as the sun went down, the ten women lit their lamps and waited by the bridegroom's front door.

And they waited.

And they waited.

And they waited.

As it got darker.

And darker.

And darker.

Soon there was no light except for a few stars and ten little flickering lamps.

"Any minute now, the bridegroom will be coming," Betty said after they had waited what seemed like a long, long time.

"Any minute now," the others agreed.

"Won't be long now," she said.

"Won't be long now," the nine answered.

"Coming soon," Betty told them.

"Coming soon," they answered.

"Look!" Betty cried out and pointed down the road. "There he is!"

She took off running and the others quickly followed.

"Welcome!" Betty sang out.

"Welcome, welcome, welcome!" the others chanted right behind her.

Then Betty stopped and bowed and said very formally, "We welcome the. . ."

"Bush," Anna said.

And Betty looked up.

Betty was bowing in front of a bush. A big bush. A bushy bush. A bush that — when it's very dark outside and you've been waiting for a long, long time — looks a lot like a bridegroom.

"Oh," said Betty. "Never mind."

So the young women walked back toward the house and sat down to wait some more. They set their lamps on the ground in front of them and pretty soon the laughing stopped and the talking stopped and their eyelids grew so, so heavy and then. . .

"Snort." One fell asleep. She sounded like a little pig grunting for its mama.

"Caw." Another couldn't keep her eyes open any longer.

"Wheeze." A third started breathing heavily in her sleep.

One by one the ten women fell asleep, their little lamps burning brightly in front of them.

Two women snorted, two went "caw," two wheezed, two went "puh-puh," and two went "woo." So they sounded like this:

"Snort."

"Caw."

"Wheeze."

"Puh-puh."

"Woo."

"Snort, caw, wheeze, puh-puh, woo."

And the longer they slept, the louder they got: "SNORT, CAW, WHEEZE, PUH-PUH, WOO! SNORT, CAW, WHEEZE, PUH-PUH, WOOOOOO!"

Until . . . "Wake up," a voice said in the darkness. "Wake up, wake up, wake up! I'm the bridegroom's servant and he is coming soon! He's almost here!"

The ten young women jumped up and it was very, very dark. Their lamps had used up all the oil and burned out. Then Anna and four other women reached into their pockets and pulled out little bottles of oil. They refilled their lamps and lit the wicks.

"Let us have some, too!" said Betty and the other four women. "We didn't bring any extra oil!"

"But, Betty," said Anna, "we may not have enough for our own lamps. Quick! Go run to the store and get some more for yourself."

So while Betty and her friends ran to the store (bumping into two trees, one big rock, and a very thorny sticker bush), the bridegroom came and Anna and her friends said, "Welcome, welcome, welcome!"

Then the bridegroom invited the five women inside with all the others who were traveling with him and he shut the big door. There were many people in the huge house listening to beautiful music, dancing, eating fine food, and drinking delicious drinks.

Later, the bridegroom was standing by the door, watching all this, when he heard a loud pounding. "Let us in! We have the oil now! We're here to welcome the bridegroom!" It was Betty and her friends. But the bridegroom said, "I don't know who you are. The young women who welcomed me are already at my party. They are having a wonderful time."

A Little Bedtime Prayer

Lord, I want to be ready like Anna and her four smart friends. I want to always welcome you into my life. And someday, Lord, I want to be in your big house at your big party. I want to dance with you. Amen.

Grown-up Stuff

This parable isn't as well known as some others and it can be hard to understand. The story can be found in Matthew (25:1-13). Jesus is reminding his followers that they must always be ready because they won't know when he is going to come again, when the end of the world is coming. And, in the same way, no one knows when he or she is going to be called home to God.

The part that's hard to understand is why the five women with extra oil didn't share with the five who didn't have any, although they did say they were afraid they might not have enough for themselves. The five smart women — wise "virgins" or "bridesmaids" in the story — don't do that because the particular quality being emphasized in this story is preparedness. Later, in the same chapter, Christ talks about how important it is to help others.

Talents for Fiddleman, Skiddleman, and Pips

Malcolm Moolah slammed the lid of his suitcase down, but he couldn't get it closed. There were just too many shirts and pants and shoes and pajamas and a little brown teddy bear he called "Malcolm Junior." This very rich man was going on a long trip and he needed to be on his way.

"You there, Fiddleman," Mr. Moolah called to one of his servants.

"And Skiddleman," he shouted to a second. "And Pips!" he yelled at a third. "Come and sit on this."

So the three servants hurried forward and plopped down on their boss's suitcase. The lid closed a little more but not enough.

"Maybe if we bounced on it?" Fiddleman said, and so the three men bounced.

And bounced.

And bounced.

But they didn't bounce at the same time. They went:

FIDDLEMAN, Skiddleman, Pips!

Fiddleman, SKIDDLEMAN, Pips!

Fiddleman, Skiddleman, PIPS!

Over and over again until finally they went:

FIDDLEMAN, SKIDDLEMAN, PIPS!

And the lid went *click!* as Mr. Moolah snapped its shiny locks.

"Gentlemen," he said to them, "I will be gone for some time and I want you to take care of a little business for me. Fiddleman?"

"Yes, Mr. Moolah." Fiddleman hopped up.

"I'm giving you five talents."

"Yes, sir, Mr. Moolah!" Fiddleman answered, knowing that even *one* talent was a coin worth a huge amount of money. "Thank you, sir!"

"Skiddleman?"

"Yes, sir." Skiddleman jumped up and stood beside Fiddleman.

"I'm giving you two talents."

"Yes, sir! Thank you, sir!"

"Pips?"

But Pips wasn't listening. He was thinking about what he was going to have for lunch.

"Pips!"

"What?" Pips asked, looking up.

"Come here," Mr. Moolah said. "I'm giving you one talent."

"Okay."

"Now," Mr. Moolah explained, "what I want each of you to do is use my money to make more money. Do you understand?"

And the three servants nodded.

As soon as Mr. Moolah was gone, Fiddleman took the five talents and he used the money very wisely and worked very hard and made five more.

Skiddleman took the two talents and he, likewise, used the money very wisely and worked very hard and made two more.

And Pips . . . Pips didn't really want to think about using the money to make more money and he certainly didn't want to work very hard. He didn't want to work much at all. So he took the one talent and went outside and dug a hole and threw the coin in. Then he covered Mr. Moolah's money with dirt and thought no more about it.

A long time later Malcolm Moolah came back from his trip and he said to his secretary, "Get me Fiddleman, Skiddleman, and Pips and get them now!"

When the three servants were standing in front of him, he said, "Gentlemen, what have you done with my money?"

"Sir," Fiddleman said. "I took your five talents and made five more for you. And here they are."

"Well done, Fiddleman," he said. "Since you did such a good job with this, I'm going to give you even more important things to do. And, by the way, I'm having a little dinner party this evening. Please be my guest."

"Yes, sir. Thank you, sir." Fiddleman said.

"Skiddleman!" Mr. Moolah said.

"Sir, I took the two talents you gave me and made you two more," Skiddleman said. "And here they are."

"Well done, Skiddleman," Mr. Moolah said. "Since you did such a good job with this, I'm going to give you even more important things to do. And, by the way, I'm having a little dinner party this evening. Please be my guest."

"Yes, sir," Skiddleman said. "Thank you, sir."

"Pips!" Mr. Moolah shouted.

"Here you go," Pips said, dropping a single coin in his boss's hand.

"What's this?"

"The talent you gave me. There might still be a little dirt on it."

"Dirt?" Mr. Moolah asked.

"Yeah. I knew your money was really important to you and you like to make a lot of it so I made sure I didn't lose it. I buried it." Pips smiled.

"You buried it?"

"Uh-huh. In the ground."

"Pips, you know I gave this to you so that you could make more money for me and you didn't even make a little more."

"At least I didn't lose it," Pips said.

"But you didn't *use* it!"

"Well," Pips said. "No. But sometimes you scare me."

"I scare you?" Mr. Moolah said and he shook his head. "And even though I scare you, you didn't do anything with the talent I gave you?"

"I dug a hole," Pips said.

"You threw my money in a hole!"

"I dug it all by myself," Pips whined.

"And left my money there."

"And I got my hands all dirty," Pips said.

"You just left that talent in the ground."

"And I remembered where I buried it," Pips said.

"I should hope so!"

"And I dug it up all by myself, too."

"Pips," Mr. Moolah said, "how do you think Fiddleman and Skiddleman made that money for me?"

Pips shrugged.

"They used the talents I gave them," Mr. Moolah said. "And they worked hard. Very hard. That's why I gave them those talents."

"So what time is the dinner party tonight?" Pips asked.

"The dinner party!" Mr. Moolah said, amazed. "You can't come to my dinner party. Here. I'm giving Fiddleman the one talent you had because he did such a good job for me. The more my servants use their talents, the more talents I will give to them. And you, Pips?"

"What?"

"Get out of here."

A Little Bedtime Prayer

Dear God, I know you're not scary like Mr. Moolah, but you've given me some treasures to use, too. Some things that I can do well. Some ways that I can help other people even though I'm still little. Thank you for these wonderful gifts. And if you ever need someone to bounce up and down on your suitcase, I'll be happy to help. Amen.

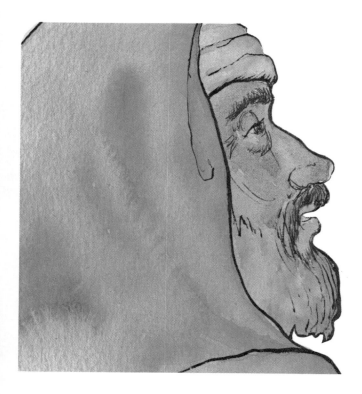

Grown-up Stuff

Jesus tells this parable (Matthew 25:14-30) right after the parable of the ten young women with the lamps. The value of the "talent" depended on whether the coin was made from gold, silver, or copper and where it was made. In any case, it was a tremendous amount of money.

But the master doesn't reward the two diligent servants with money. He refers to that as "small matters." Instead he promises to give them "greater responsibilities" and asks them to "come, share your master's joy." He is welcoming them to be a part of his kingdom.

Jesus is telling us how we can be a part of God's kingdom.

Young children try hard to make certain life is fair — everyone gets the same number of cookies or gets a turn picking which cartoon show will be watched — but the master in Christ's parable gives different amounts. The point is not who gets what but what each servant does with whatever amount he is given. The third man is not punished because he does not make five or two talents but because he does not use the single talent he is given. It is his fear and laziness that keep him from the kingdom.

In real life, only I know how many talents God has given me and it's up to me to discover what they are and how to use them wisely.

Patrick, the Prodigal Son

"Cock-a-doodle-doo!" a rooster crowed loudly, and young Patrick buried his head under his pillow. Morning? Already? But he was *so* tired.

He heard his older brother, John, getting up from his own bed and getting dressed. "Come on, Pat," John said and gave him a nudge. "Lots to do today."

"Lots to do today," Patrick repeated. "Lots to do. Lots to do." He pulled the pillow off and said, "Maybe today I don't want to do lots? Did you ever think of that?"

But John just laughed and headed to the kitchen for breakfast. "Good morning," Patrick heard him say to their father. "It's a beautiful morning!" he heard their father answer.

"Cock-a-doodle-doo!" the rooster crowed again. Was it right outside his window? He'd teach that stupid bird a lesson. Patrick scooped up one of his shoes and went to the window.

"Where are you?" he called out. "I've got a surprise for you."

The sun was just coming up over one of the barns. His father had several barns. And a lot of land. And a huge number of sheep and goats and cattle. His brother had been right. There *was* lots to do today. A lot of work with all those barns and land and animals.

But Patrick was thinking about only one animal: an eight-pound chicken that woke him up every morning.

"Cock-a-doodle. . ." the rooster began to cry out when Patrick threw the shoe as hard as he could. "Rawk!" screeched the rooster and jumped away.

"Gotcha!" Patrick yelled.

"Rawk!" the rooster complained as it ran and fluttered and flew away from the house.

"I've got one more shoe!" Patrick warned it.

"Rawk!" the rooster screeched once more and was gone.

"You're so lucky," Patrick said. "You can get away from here. You can go anywhere you want. You can. . ." Suddenly he stopped talking. He thought about what he had said. If a rooster could do it, why couldn't he?

Patrick got dressed quickly and went to the kitchen. His father was sitting alone at the table. His older brother had already gone out to begin working.

"Pop," Patrick said, "all these barns and land and animals are worth a lot of money, aren't they?"

His father nodded.

"And when you die. . ." Patrick began.

"When I die!" his father said and laughed. "That's what we're going to talk about at the breakfast table?"

"I mean, when you die a long time from now, then half of all this will be mine and half will be John's, right?"

"That's right."

"Well," Patrick said. "I want my half now."

His father looked sad. "Why?" he asked his son.

"It will be mine someday, right? Well, I want it now."

So his father divided all the property and Patrick quickly sold everything his father gave him. A few days later he took a big bag of money and headed out the door. He went on a long trip to a faraway country and he ate whatever he wanted to eat and he drank whatever he wanted to drink and he did whatever he wanted to do. Patrick had become a prodigal son. A person who is prodigal is one who spends and spends and spends.

But it wasn't very long before Patrick's big bag of money was empty. He had no way to buy food or drink or a place to stay. "I need some money," he said to himself. "I need a job."

But there weren't many jobs in that faraway country and there wasn't much food for any of the people because the crops weren't growing well. So he hunted and hunted for a job until finally a farmer told him, "You can feed my pigs. That will be your job."

After that, Patrick would spend his days feeding the pigs and he would get so hungry that even the pigs' food looked good. In fact, it looked more than good. It looked *wonderful.* "You never share with me," he said to the animals. "You pigs are such . . . pigs." But the pigs just answered, "Grunt, grunt, grunt."

"I wish I could have some of your food," he told them. "You're so lucky."

Then he remembered the rooster. And his father's barns, land, and other animals. He remembered his father.

"What am I doing here!" he cried out to the pigs. "Even the servants who work for Pop eat better than I do. I can go back to him. I'll say, 'Pop, I made a big mistake and

I'm sorry. I don't deserve to be your son, but please let me be one of your servants.'"

"Grunt, grunt, grunt," the pigs answered, but he didn't hear them. He was already beginning his long journey back to his father's farm.

Later, when Patrick was still a ways from his old house, his father saw him coming down the road and felt so sorry for him. The father ran all the way to meet him and gave his boy a big hug and kiss.

"Pop," Patrick began, trying to remember how he had practiced what he was going to say. But instead, he started to cry. "Papa," he said. "I was wrong. I'm sorry. I don't deserve to be your son, but. . ."

"Quick!" the father called out to his servants. "Get the best clothes from the house! And shoes! And a ring for his finger! Take that special calf and get it ready for a giant barbecue! We're going to celebrate because it was like my son was dead, but now he's come back to life! He was lost, but now he's been found!"

Then the party *really* began.

A little while later the older son, John, was coming in from working in one of the fields and he heard the music and smelled the barbecue and saw all the people dancing, so he called out to a servant, "What's going on?"

"Your brother is back!" the servant said. "Your father killed that special calf and there's a big party because Patrick came back to him safe and sound."

That made John *very* mad. He wouldn't even go near the house, so his father came out and begged him to come see his brother.

"It's not fair," John complained. "I worked hard for you all these years and I never disobeyed you and you never even killed a goat for my friends and me. But Patrick comes back after wasting all your money and you have this big party for him!"

"Johnny," the father said softly as he held his son's face between his hands and looked him straight in the eyes. "You're always here with me. Everything I have, you have. It's all yours."

John thought about that.

"Come on," the father said, reaching down and taking his older son by the hand. "Let's go celebrate. I didn't just get a son back. You got a brother. Your brother was dead, but he's come back to life. He was lost, but now we've found him."

A Little Bedtime Prayer

Heavenly Father, you're always there to welcome me with a big hug. All the

good things that you have you want me to have, too. Thank you. And I'm never going to throw my shoe at a rooster. Amen.

Grown-up Stuff

This very famous parable can be found in Luke 15:11-32. (Right after the story of the one hundred sheep and the story of the lost coin.) In it, the father doesn't just forgive his younger son; he's been watching for the boy's return and rushes out to welcome him back. The son doesn't even finish admitting he has done wrong before the father embraces him and accepts him, not as a servant, but as a member of the family. The father is so filled with joy that he calls for a celebration.

It's easy to forget the older son, but he's important, too. At one time or another we all complain at how unfair life seems to be because we fail to see and appreciate all that we have. In Jesus' story, again the father comes out to one of his children and gently invites the son to go to the party with him.

In the same way, God is always inviting each of us — preschoolers, parents, grandparents, and everyone else — to be a part of his kingdom, inviting each of us to the celebration that will never end.